MAYER SMITH

In the Shadows of Her Fortune

Copyright © 2025 by Mayer Smith

All rights reserved. No part of this publication may be reproduced, stored or transmitted in any form or by any means, electronic, mechanical, photocopying, recording, scanning, or otherwise without written permission from the publisher. It is illegal to copy this book, post it to a website, or distribute it by any other means without permission.

This novel is entirely a work of fiction. The names, characters and incidents portrayed in it are the work of the author's imagination. Any resemblance to actual persons, living or dead, events or localities is entirely coincidental.

Mayer Smith asserts the moral right to be identified as the author of this work.

Mayer Smith has no responsibility for the persistence or accuracy of URLs for external or third-party Internet Websites referred to in this publication and does not guarantee that any content on such Websites is, or will remain, accurate or appropriate.

Designations used by companies to distinguish their products are often claimed as trademarks. All brand names and product names used in this book and on its cover are trade names, service marks, trademarks and registered trademarks of their respective owners. The publishers and the book are not associated with any product or vendor mentioned in this book. None of the companies referenced within the book have endorsed the book.

First edition

This book was professionally typeset on Reedsy. Find out more at reedsy.com

Contents

1	The Silent Heiress	1
2	A New Identity	7
3	The Charming Stranger	13
4	Secrets and Lies	19
5	The Fortune Hunter	25
6	Growing Closer	32
7	The Truth Unveiled	39
8	The Conflict of Worlds	45
9	A Test of Love	52
10	The Burden of Wealth	59
11	A Chance Encounter	65
12	Rebuilding Trust	72
13	The Shadows Linger	79
14	Letting Go	86
15	Embracing Her True Self	93

One

The Silent Heiress

Vivienne Hart sat at the grand window of her penthouse, staring out at the sprawling city below. The lights twinkled like a million tiny stars, each one a reminder of the life she had carefully constructed, a life she was now desperate to leave behind. She ran her fingers along the cool glass, tracing the outline of the skyline. To anyone else, it might have seemed like an image of perfection—an empire of wealth, power, and influence—but to Vivienne, it was a gilded cage.

For years, she had been the heiress to the Hart fortune, a sprawling estate of business ventures that spanned continents, an inheritance passed down through generations, and a name that commanded attention the world over. At twenty-eight, she was already a force to be reckoned with. Boardrooms cowered under her presence, investors sought her out, and the media constantly speculated about her every move. But none of it mattered to Vivienne anymore.

The weight of her wealth was suffocating. The pressure to maintain the family legacy, the constant prying eyes of the press, and the unspoken expectation that she would settle into her role as a flawless icon—none of it was what she wanted. For years, she had played the part with grace, always the perfect picture of success, always the woman everyone wanted to be. But she had grown tired of it. She was tired of being seen as nothing more than an extension of her family's fortune, an object to be admired, but never truly known.

Her reflection stared back at her from the window, a woman draped in designer clothes, her hair perfectly styled, her face sculpted to the point of perfection. She didn't recognize the woman in the glass anymore. She had become so far removed from herself that the reflection seemed almost like a stranger. A mask.

And that mask was about to come off.

The thought had consumed her for months, a quiet whisper in the back of her mind that she couldn't shake. It had started as a mere fantasy, a dream of escape, but now it was an overwhelming desire to break free. She had everything she could ever want—money, status, adoration—but none of it filled the emptiness inside her. What good was it to have the world at your feet if you could never experience life on your own terms? If you could never be loved for who you truly were, not what you represented?

Vivienne's fingers tightened on the glass, a subtle tremor passing through her body. She had made a decision. The decision to leave it all behind.

The plan had been in the works for weeks. She would disappear. She would walk away from her family's empire, her lavish lifestyle, and everything that came with it. The world would think she had simply vanished, a reclusive heiress choosing to fade into obscurity. But the truth was far more complicated. Vivienne didn't just want to disappear—she wanted to test herself. She wanted to know if love, real love, was possible outside the fortress of her wealth. Could someone love her for the woman she truly was, or would they only be drawn to the fortune that lingered in the background of every interaction?

Her eyes flicked to the clock on the wall. In a few hours, the world would begin to notice her absence. The press would speculate about her sudden disappearance, and her family would be forced to put out some kind of statement. They would demand answers. But Vivienne had made up her mind. She didn't care what they thought. This was her life, and it was time for her to take control.

She turned away from the window and glanced at the sleek black suitcase sitting on the floor at the foot of her bed. Inside, she had packed only the essentials: a few changes of clothes, her passport, some cash, and the bare minimum to start a new life. There was no room for excess. She didn't need luxury. She didn't need the extravagant comforts that had always been her norm. What she needed was freedom—the freedom to find out who she really was, away from the watchful eyes of her family, away from the expectations of the world.

Vivienne stood up and walked to the suitcase. She hesitated for a moment, her fingers resting on the zipper. Could she really go through with it? Could she leave everything behind, knowing she would never be able to return? The life she had built—the house, the cars, the clothes, the people—would it all just be a memory?

But then she remembered the feeling that had been growing inside her, the sense of suffocation that had steadily built over the years. The pressure to live up to her family's legacy had become unbearable. She had never asked for any of it. All she had ever wanted was to be seen as more than the sum of her wealth.

Her decision was final. She zipped up the suitcase, grabbed her keys, and walked out of the penthouse, leaving behind the only world she had ever known.

—-

The taxi ride to the airport was uneventful. Vivienne sat in the back, her eyes fixed on the city passing by. It felt surreal, as though she were watching someone else's life unfold before her. There was no going back now. As the car pulled up to the terminal, her heart raced, and she couldn't help but feel a strange mixture of excitement and fear.

She stepped out of the cab, her heels clicking on the polished floor of the airport. She kept her head down, avoiding eye

The Silent Heiress

contact with anyone around her. Her dark sunglasses shielded her eyes, and her simple black dress made her look like any other traveler. She had left the glamour behind. In this moment, she was just another woman, traveling alone, with nothing but a suitcase and a new identity.

Vivienne handed her passport to the attendant at the counter, her hands steady despite the storm of emotions brewing inside her. She was just another face in the crowd, unremarkable. No one here knew her name, her wealth, or her family's legacy. She could be anyone. And that's exactly what she wanted.

The flight was long, but her mind was consumed by the thought of what lay ahead. A new life. A new beginning. She would have to be careful. She couldn't let anyone—especially Alex—discover who she really was. She had to remain in the shadows, hidden behind the life she had chosen.

When the plane touched down, Vivienne stepped off and took a deep breath of the unfamiliar air. She had no destination in mind, just a need to be anonymous, to be free. For the first time in years, she felt a spark of hope. Maybe, just maybe, this was the beginning of something she had never allowed herself to believe in: the possibility of real love, without the weight of her fortune to distort it.

But Vivienne knew that her true test was only beginning. How long could she keep her secret? How long could she hide in the shadows before the truth came to light?

As she walked away from the terminal, a single thought echoed in her mind: The journey ahead would not be easy, but it would be worth it. For the first time in years, she was living for herself. And that, she knew, was the greatest fortune of all.

Two

A New Identity

Vivienne's new life began in a small town nestled on the edge of the coast, far from the bustling metropolis that had once been her domain. She arrived late in the evening, the streets eerily quiet except for the occasional rustle of wind in the trees. The town, like its inhabitants, seemed content in its own slow pace, unaffected by the rush of the outside world. It was exactly what Vivienne needed: a sanctuary, a place where she could breathe again.

The town was picturesque, its streets lined with old brick buildings and cozy cottages, the kind that looked like they belonged in a time long past. The air was fresh, filled with the scent of saltwater and earth. Vivienne felt the tension in her chest ease slightly as she walked along the cobblestone path leading to the small inn where she had booked a room for the night. The light above the door flickered in the breeze, casting long shadows over the entryway.

The inn was modest, nothing like the luxury hotels she was accustomed to, but it had its own charm. It was quaint, warm, and homely, a stark contrast to the opulent hotels and resorts she had grown up in. A sense of comfort washed over her as she stepped inside. The lobby was dimly lit, with a fireplace crackling gently on one side. Behind the counter stood a middle-aged woman with a friendly smile, her graying hair tied in a loose bun.

"Good evening," Vivienne said, her voice steady but softer than usual. She had always been used to commanding attention, but here, in this quiet town, she had to adjust her tone. No one would know her name. No one would know who she was.

"Welcome," the woman replied, her voice warm and welcoming. "Do you have a reservation?"

Vivienne nodded and handed over her ID, which now read 'Vera Hall,' a name she had chosen carefully, far removed from her former identity. She had spent days researching common names in small towns like this one, choosing one that felt both ordinary and unremarkable. "Yes, it's under Vera Hall."

The woman glanced down at the register, then back up at Vivienne with a knowing smile. "Ah, yes. Your room is ready. We have a lovely view of the ocean." She handed Vivienne a key, the metal cool in her hand. "Room 12. If you need anything, just let me know."

A New Identity

Vivienne thanked her and made her way to the staircase, her footsteps light on the wooden steps. Her mind was racing, still adjusting to the weight of her decision. The world she had left behind was distant now, but the echoes of it still lingered. She couldn't help but wonder if she had made the right choice. Could she really disappear into this simple life? Could she hide here, among these people, and leave her past behind?

As she opened the door to her room, a wave of exhaustion hit her. The space was small, but comfortable. A large bed with white linens sat against the wall, next to a window that framed the view of the dark, churning sea. The sound of the waves crashing against the rocks below was soothing, almost hypnotic. She could hear the faint call of seagulls in the distance, adding to the peaceful atmosphere.

Vivienne set her suitcase on the bed and walked over to the window. She let out a deep breath, feeling the cool air brush her skin as she looked out at the endless horizon. For the first time in a long while, she felt like she could finally breathe. The life she had left behind—her family, her fortune, her responsibilities— seemed so distant now, like it belonged to someone else.

But the weight of her secret still hung over her. She was Vera Hall now. There was no turning back. She had to commit to this new identity, to this new life. The shadows of her past would always be with her, but she couldn't let them dictate her future.

The next morning, Vivienne—now Vera—woke up early, the soft light of dawn filtering through the curtains. She dressed quickly in a simple blouse and jeans, taking care to keep her appearance low-key. She had learned long ago that her looks were one of her greatest assets—and one of her greatest liabilities. In her old life, her beauty had been a tool, something that opened doors and garnered attention. But here, in this town, she needed to blend in. She wasn't Vera Hall the heiress; she was just another woman trying to find her way.

After a quick breakfast in the inn's small dining room, Vivienne decided to explore the town. She had no particular destination in mind, but she wanted to get a feel for the place. The streets were quieter in the morning, with only a few locals going about their business. The café on the corner caught her eye, its windows fogged from the warmth inside. She walked in, drawn to the smell of fresh coffee and baked goods.

The café was a charming little spot, with mismatched tables and chairs scattered around. The walls were adorned with local art, and the hum of conversation filled the air. Vivienne approached the counter, where a young woman with short brown hair was busy arranging pastries.

"Good morning," Vivienne said, her voice soft but clear. "I'll have a cappuccino, please."

The woman smiled warmly, her eyes taking in Vivienne's appearance. "Sure, coming right up. First time in town?"

Vivienne nodded, feeling the weight of her answer. "Yes, just moved here."

A New Identity

The woman raised an eyebrow in curiosity, but said nothing more, simply handing Vivienne her cappuccino. "Well, welcome. I'm Alex. If you need any recommendations, just ask."

Vivienne took the cup, feeling the warmth of the ceramic against her hand. She made her way to a small table by the window, her eyes scanning the room. People came and went, each one going about their day in their own way, oblivious to the woman who sat among them, carrying the weight of a secret too heavy to bear.

It wasn't long before the door opened again, and a man walked in. He was tall, with dark hair and an easy smile. He wore a worn leather jacket and jeans, his boots scuffing softly on the wooden floor as he made his way to the counter. Vivienne couldn't help but glance up, drawn to the ease with which he carried himself. He had the look of someone who belonged here, someone who knew the rhythm of this place.

"Morning, Alex," the man said, his voice deep and familiar. He nodded in Vivienne's direction, as if noticing her for the first time. "What's new?"

"Not much," Alex replied, wiping her hands on a towel. "Just another day in paradise."

The man laughed and turned his attention to Vivienne. "You're new here, right?"

Vivienne's heart skipped a beat. She nodded, trying to maintain her composure. "Yes, I'm just settling in."

"I'm Ethan," the man said, extending his hand. "Nice to meet you. You're in for a treat around here. It's a quiet town, but it has its charm."

Vivienne shook his hand, surprised by the warmth of his touch. There was something about Ethan that felt different, something that made her heart flutter in a way she hadn't expected. She hadn't planned on meeting anyone here, hadn't planned on being noticed, but here she was, already making a connection.

"I'm Vera," she said, her voice steady despite the whirlwind of emotions inside her. "I'm just getting to know the place."

Ethan's smile widened, and for a moment, Vivienne felt as though she were looking into the eyes of someone who could see through the layers of her disguise. She quickly looked away, afraid of what might happen if he saw too much. But she couldn't shake the feeling that this encounter was no coincidence.

As the morning wore on, Vivienne couldn't help but think about Ethan. There was something about him, something that stirred a curiosity she hadn't felt in years. But the question lingered in the back of her mind: how long could she hide? How long could she remain in the shadows of her own life, pretending to be someone she was not?

Three

The Charming Stranger

The town felt more like home with each passing day, its gentle pace gradually working its way into Vivienne's heart. Yet, no matter how much she tried to blend in, her past loomed over her like a shadow she could never escape. It was only a matter of time before someone would come too close to discovering who she really was. And that thought gnawed at her, reminding her that she could never truly be free—not as long as she kept her secret.

The days were simple and predictable. Vivienne—Vera—spent her mornings at the café, chatting with Alex when she had the chance, and quietly sipping her cappuccinos, watching the steady rhythm of life around her. The evenings were filled with walks along the shoreline, the sound of the waves crashing against the rocks like a lullaby. For a brief moment, she felt at peace, like she was finally living for herself instead of for everyone else. The ache in her chest that had been with her for so long began to dull, replaced by the sense of freedom she had desperately sought.

But beneath the surface of this quiet life, there were things stirring. Ethan, the man who had greeted her on that first day in the café, was beginning to occupy more of her thoughts. She had tried to keep her distance, telling herself that she was simply getting to know the locals. He was charming, easy to talk to, and had a way of making her feel like she belonged in this small town. But she couldn't allow herself to get too close. She couldn't risk it.

One evening, as she walked along the beach just as the sun began to set, she heard footsteps behind her. She knew who it was before she turned around. Ethan's figure emerged from the shadows, his silhouette dark against the fading light.

"You're here early," Vivienne said, forcing a smile as he drew near. The cool air blew her hair back from her face, but she didn't dare touch it, not wanting to draw attention to herself. She had worked so hard to shed the layers of wealth and glamour that had defined her.

"I couldn't sleep," Ethan replied, his voice carrying the familiarity of someone who had long since abandoned pretenses. He stopped beside her, glancing out at the ocean. "Something about the sound of the waves… it's calming."

Vivienne nodded, her gaze fixed on the horizon. She had heard those same words in a hundred different ways from strangers she'd met over the years. It was one of the reasons she had never felt truly seen. People saw only what they wanted to see—the heiress, the businesswoman, the woman of mystery. No one ever truly understood her, and that was exactly how she liked it. But Ethan… Ethan made her feel like she could be herself—like she didn't have to pretend.

"You know, Vera," Ethan began, breaking her train of thought, "I've been thinking. You've been here a while now, and I've gotten to know you a bit, but there's something about you. Something doesn't quite add up."

Vivienne's heart skipped a beat. His words hung in the air like a warning bell, the subtle edge to his voice sending a chill down her spine. He hadn't raised his voice, but there was no mistaking the curiosity in his tone. The suspicion.

"What do you mean?" Vivienne asked, her voice betraying nothing. She turned to face him, but kept her posture neutral, carefully controlled. She had to maintain her distance.

"You've got that… air about you," Ethan said, his eyes scanning her face as though trying to unravel some hidden mystery. "You're not like the rest of the town. I mean, you're not from here, right?"

Vivienne felt her throat tighten, the panic threatening to rise. She had known this day would come, but she hadn't expected it to happen so soon, or with him. Ethan, the one person she had let her guard down around, the one person she had started to feel comfortable with. But now that comfort felt like a trap.

"I'm from..." she hesitated, searching for something that sounded real enough, something that wouldn't give her away. "I'm from a few towns over. It's... been a while since I've been in a place like this."

Ethan nodded slowly, but he didn't seem convinced. "Right. But I've been around this town long enough to know that people who come here usually have something they're running from." He stepped closer, his eyes narrowing as he studied her. "You don't talk much about your past. You don't even talk about your family. And the way you carry yourself... it's not like the rest of us."

Vivienne's chest tightened. She could feel her pulse pounding in her ears, the blood rushing to her head. Ethan wasn't letting up. His gaze was sharp, probing, as though he could see right through her carefully constructed façade.

"I don't have a family," she said quickly, hoping to end the conversation before it got any further. "I'm just... just looking for a fresh start."

Ethan's expression softened, but there was still a glint of doubt in his eyes. "Fresh start, huh? I get that. But people don't just pick up and leave everything behind without a reason. There's always something they're hiding."

Vivienne didn't answer. She couldn't. She couldn't allow herself to get tangled in a web of lies. But she couldn't let the truth slip, either. The truth that would expose everything she had fought so hard to bury.

Ethan studied her for a long moment, and then, to her surprise, he stepped back. "You don't have to tell me everything," he said quietly. "I'm not trying to force you into anything, but if you ever feel like talking... I'm here."

Vivienne nodded, relief flooding her chest. But as Ethan turned to walk away, she couldn't shake the feeling that he was still watching her, still wondering what lay behind the mask she had put on. She could feel his eyes on her back, the unspoken question hanging between them.

The following days passed in a blur. Vivienne kept to her routine, working at the café during the day and walking along the beach in the evenings. But the tension that had been building between her and Ethan gnawed at her, threatening to unravel everything she had worked so hard to build. He was close to discovering her secret, and every time she saw him, every time they spoke, the weight of her lie grew heavier.

She knew she couldn't keep hiding forever. Sooner or later, someone would figure out who she really was. And when they did, what would become of her? Would Ethan still look at her the same way, or would he see her as just another wealthy woman, hiding behind a disguise?

It was a Saturday afternoon when everything came to a head. Vivienne had just finished her shift at the café when she noticed Ethan sitting at a table near the window, his eyes focused on something just outside. She approached him slowly, her footsteps hesitant. She had to know if he had figured it out. She had to know if he could see through her lies.

"Ethan," she said, her voice quieter than usual. She wasn't sure if it was the weight of her own thoughts or the apprehension in her chest, but she couldn't bring herself to speak louder.

He looked up from his cup of coffee, his eyes locking onto hers. There was something different in his gaze now—something that made Vivienne's stomach tighten.

"Vera," he said, his voice low. "I've been thinking."

Vivienne's breath hitched. "About what?"

"You." He paused, watching her carefully. "About the way you've been acting, the way you disappear every time someone mentions the town's history, or your past. You're hiding something, Vera. And it's eating away at you."

She froze. His words were like a dagger, slicing through the fragile web of lies she had spun around herself. She didn't know what to say. The truth was out there now, but she still didn't know if she was ready to face it.

"Ethan, please…" Vivienne whispered, her voice cracking. The walls she had spent so long building began to crumble, and for the first time since she'd arrived in this town, she realized there might be no way to escape the truth.

Four

Secrets and Lies

Vivienne felt as if the ground had slipped away from beneath her, and for a moment, all she could do was stand there, her breath shallow and her heart hammering in her chest. Ethan's words had torn through the fragile barrier she had spent weeks constructing. She had always been good at hiding the truth and wearing the mask of Vera Hall, the woman with no past. But now, staring into Ethan's unwavering gaze, she realized how close she had come to losing everything. She was close to revealing the one thing she had fought so hard to bury.

She hadn't planned on telling anyone. She hadn't planned on getting close to anyone. The last thing she had wanted was for anyone to see her, to know her for who she indeed was. But Ethan... Ethan was different. He wasn't just some passing stranger; he had a way of seeing through the layers she'd wrapped around herself, and that terrified her.

"I'm not hiding anything," she said, her voice a little too sharp, a little too defensive. She forced a smile, trying to ignore the pounding of her heart in her ears. "I don't know what you think you've figured out, but you're wrong."

Ethan leaned back in his chair, his eyes never leaving hers. He didn't look angry, or accusatory—just calm. Too calm.

"I don't think you're hiding anything, Vera," he said, his voice steady, almost soothing. "I think you're running from something."

Vivienne felt the blood drain from her face. She wanted to argue, to deny it all, but the words felt like they were trapped in her throat. He was right. She was running. She had been running for years, from the pressures of her family, from the suffocating weight of her fortune, from the life that had been forced upon her. But she wasn't ready to confront that yet—not with him, not now.

"I'm not running from anything," she managed to say, though her voice wavered. "I'm just looking for a peaceful life. Is that so hard to understand?"

Ethan studied her, his expression unreadable. He seemed to be weighing something in his mind, deciding whether to push further or let her retreat. After what felt like an eternity, he leaned forward slightly, his voice soft but firm.

"Vera, it's not about what you say. It's about what you don't say. I can see it in the way you act, the way you avoid talking about yourself. It's in the way you carry yourself, like you're carrying a secret you don't want anyone to know."

Vivienne swallowed, her throat dry. She had thought she could escape. She had thought that by changing her name, by walking away from her old life, she could leave her past behind. But Ethan was right. It wasn't just her name she had changed—it was the very way she moved through the world. She had built a wall around herself, brick by brick, each layer of falsehood making her feel safer, more hidden from the truth. But in doing so, she had forgotten how to truly connect with others.

She could feel her resolve starting to crack. She had spent so many years pretending, so many years convincing herself that if she could just stay hidden long enough, the past would be forgotten. But Ethan's words were like a mirror, reflecting back the parts of herself she had tried so desperately to leave behind.

"Why does it matter?" she asked, her voice barely above a whisper. She wasn't sure if she was asking him or herself. "Why does it matter what I'm hiding? I'm here, I'm living a simple life. That's all you need to know."

Ethan didn't answer right away. He just sat there, looking at her with a mixture of sympathy and curiosity. His eyes softened slightly, but there was a glint of something else behind them—something deeper. "It matters because I think you're running from more than just your past. I think you're running from yourself."

Vivienne felt the walls closing in around her. She could feel the pressure building, the weight of everything she had kept buried for so long threatening to explode. She had been so careful, so meticulous in her efforts to keep the truth hidden, but now it seemed like everything was unraveling, like the very act of living in the shadows was starting to pull her under.

"You don't know me, Ethan," she said, her voice rising with a mix of frustration and fear. "You don't know what I've been through. You don't know what it's like to be suffocated by the weight of your own name, to be trapped by expectations that have nothing to do with who you actually are."

Ethan didn't flinch. He didn't back away. He just watched her, his expression softening further. "I don't know your story, Vera. But I want to. I want to understand why you're so afraid of being who you really are."

Her breath caught in her throat. The question hung in the air between them, and for the first time, Vivienne felt the weight of the lie she had been living. She had spent so many years hiding from the truth that she had forgotten what it felt like to be seen, to be known for who she truly was.

The silence stretched on, thick and suffocating. Vivienne's mind raced, torn between the need to protect herself and the overwhelming desire to finally open up, to let someone see her for who she was. But the fear of what that would mean, the fear of what Ethan might think if he knew the truth, held her in place.

Ethan leaned back in his chair, his eyes never leaving her. "You don't have to tell me everything," he said quietly. "But I can't keep pretending like I don't see what's happening here. You're not the person you're pretending to be, Vera. And I think you know that."

Vivienne's hands clenched into fists at her sides, her nails digging into her palms. She didn't want to admit it. She didn't want to admit that she had spent years running from the truth, from the very thing that had shaped her. The truth about her family, about the legacy that weighed on her every decision, about the love that had never truly been hers to begin with.

Her eyes burned, and she quickly blinked back the tears that threatened to fall. She wouldn't let herself break down, not here, not now. She had already lost so much. She couldn't afford to lose this too.

"I don't want to talk about it," she said, her voice barely above a whisper. She turned away from him, her heart pounding in her chest. "I just want to be left alone."

Ethan didn't respond immediately. For a long moment, the only sound was the soft murmur of conversation from the other tables in the café. Then, slowly, he stood up. His movement was slow and deliberate, but there was a quiet resolve in his actions.

"I'm not going anywhere, Vera," he said softly. "Whenever you're ready to talk, I'll be here. But you can't keep running forever."

Vivienne's breath hitched as she watched him turn and walk away. The door chimed softly as he left, and for the first time since she'd arrived in this town, Vivienne felt completely, utterly alone.

She sank into the chair he had just vacated, her hands trembling. The weight of her past pressed down on her, suffocating her in a way she had never experienced before. She had spent so many years running from it, pretending it didn't matter, but now it was here, standing in front of her. And she couldn't outrun it any longer.

The town, the peaceful life she had tried to build, suddenly felt like a prison. The shadows she had been hiding in were closing in around her, and she realized, with a sinking feeling, that no matter how far she ran, no matter how many miles she put between herself and her past, the truth would always be with her. It was a part of her. And sooner or later, someone would find it.

But the question was, when they did—when Ethan discovered the truth—would he still be there? Or would he walk away, just like everyone else had when they learned who she really was?

Five

The Fortune Hunter

The day after Ethan's words hung heavily in Vivienne's mind. His insistence that she was hiding from herself had struck a nerve she wasn't prepared to face. The reality of his gaze, steady and probing, had made her feel like the walls she had spent years building around herself were made of paper, easily torn apart by the gentlest touch. She had managed to convince herself that she was safe here, that in this small town, she could finally shed the weight of her past. But now, with every passing moment, it felt like her secret was slipping from her grasp, slipping into the hands of someone who might understand too much.

The morning after their conversation, Vivienne stayed in bed longer than usual, staring at the ceiling, her thoughts tangled in a web of doubts and fear. The cottage she had rented for the past few weeks had become both a sanctuary and a prison, and every creak of the wooden floors, every whisper of wind against the window, felt like a reminder of how fragile her peace really was.

The simple life she had envisioned for herself in this quiet corner of the world felt increasingly like an illusion, and Ethan was the reason. She couldn't ignore the way he looked at her, like he could see through the layers of her carefully constructed persona. She had never been so exposed in her life. No one had ever questioned her so directly, not in a way that made her feel like she was running out of time.

By the time the sun had risen high in the sky, Vivienne couldn't avoid it any longer. She needed to face the truth, even if she wasn't ready to speak it aloud. She had to leave the safety of her cottage, step into the world she had been trying to avoid, and face the consequences of her choices. Her heart pounded as she dressed quickly, pulling on a loose blouse and jeans, the same simple clothes she had grown accustomed to wearing.

The streets of the town were quiet in the early hours of the morning, just the hum of distant voices and the soft chirping of birds filling the air. The café was already open when she arrived, the door jingling as she stepped inside. Alex was behind the counter, making fresh coffee, his back turned to her as she walked in. Vivienne had hoped to avoid any interaction today, to lose herself in the routine that had been her refuge, but something about the place, something about the comforting smell of freshly brewed coffee, called to her. It grounded her, even if only for a moment.

"Morning, Vera," Alex said without turning around, as he poured the steaming coffee into a mug. "You're up early today."

Vivienne smiled, though it didn't quite reach her eyes. "I couldn't sleep."

"Bad dreams?" he asked, finally turning to face her. His gaze was warm, his eyes kind, but there was a glint of curiosity behind them, as if he could sense that something was off.

Vivienne hesitated, unsure of how much to reveal. She had been careful with Alex, just as she had with everyone else in town. But something about the way he looked at her now made her feel like he might be able to see the cracks in her facade, even without knowing the full story.

"Something like that," she replied with a nonchalant shrug, trying to dismiss the gnawing feeling that was settling in her chest.

Alex didn't push any further. He simply placed a cup of coffee on the counter and slid it toward her. "You're not the only one who's had bad nights, you know. We all have our demons."

The comment struck a chord with Vivienne, and she found herself nodding. Demons. That was exactly what she had—her past, her family, the lie she had built her life around. But no one here knew about it. No one knew who she really was, and that, for a moment, made her feel like she might be able to breathe again.

In the Shadows of Her Fortune

She took the coffee, savoring the warmth of it as she walked to the small table by the window, settling into a seat that had become familiar. The town was still quiet, the world moving slowly around her, and for a few minutes, Vivienne allowed herself to pretend that she had the luxury of time.

But as she sipped the coffee, her thoughts drifted back to Ethan. His words echoed in her mind—You're running from something. She didn't want to admit it, but deep down, she knew he was right. She had been running her entire life. Running from the expectations of her family, running from the pressure to live up to her inheritance, running from the fact that her life had never been her own. And now, running from him, from the very man who had come closest to seeing her for who she really was.

Suddenly, a shadow passed over her table, and she looked up to find Ethan standing in front of her, his hands tucked into his jacket pockets. He looked just as calm as he had the day before, but there was a tension in his posture that hadn't been there before.

"Mind if I join you?" he asked, his voice casual, but his eyes searching hers for an answer she wasn't ready to give.

Vivienne felt her pulse quicken. She opened her mouth to say something, anything, but found that the words wouldn't come. He was here, standing in front of her, and she was more afraid than she had ever been.

"I—" She cleared her throat, trying to steady herself. "Sure. But, uh, I don't have much to offer."

Ethan sat down without waiting for an invitation. He didn't seem to mind the awkwardness in the air; instead, he watched her carefully, his expression unreadable.

"So," he said after a moment, his voice low but purposeful, "about yesterday."

Vivienne felt a knot form in her stomach. She had hoped he would let it go, that the silence between them would speak louder than anything she could say. But she knew he wouldn't back down. Ethan wasn't the kind of man who would walk away from an unfinished conversation. And for reasons she couldn't quite explain, part of her didn't want him to.

"What about yesterday?" she asked, her voice colder than she intended. She couldn't help it—her guard was up now, her walls higher than ever. She had to protect herself, had to keep him at arm's length, no matter how badly she wanted to break down the barriers.

"You said you were running from something," Ethan said, his tone steady, "and I think I know what it is."

Vivienne stiffened, her heart pounding in her chest. She couldn't breathe. How could he know? Had he figured it out? Had her carefully crafted facade cracked so easily? She gripped the edge of her coffee cup, trying to steady herself, to keep her composure.

"I don't know what you're talking about," she said, but even as the words left her mouth, she knew they sounded hollow.

Ethan leaned forward slightly, his eyes softening, as though he could sense her unease. "Vera, I don't want to push you. But I think you need someone to talk to. And I think you're more connected to this place than you realize."

Vivienne blinked, unsure of what he meant by his words. More connected? What did that mean? Was he just guessing, or had he somehow seen through her carefully constructed layers?

"You don't know me," she said, her voice firmer now, though a part of her was beginning to feel that familiar ache of fear rising again.

Ethan didn't respond immediately. He seemed to be considering something, watching her closely, as if trying to read the unspoken truth in her eyes. "Maybe not. But I'm starting to understand more than you think. There's a connection here, Vera. A connection you're trying so hard to avoid."

Vivienne's breath caught in her throat. The unspoken words hung in the air between them, and she realized, for the first time, that Ethan wasn't just talking about the town. He wasn't just talking about her past. He was talking about the invisible thread that tied them together in ways she couldn't yet comprehend, but which she couldn't deny either.

The connection was there. She could feel it, a pull that she hadn't expected, a magnetic force drawing them together despite the walls she had put up. And for the first time since arriving in this town, Vivienne felt the weight of her secret, the weight of the truth she had been running from, begin to shift.

But she wasn't ready to face it. Not yet. Not with Ethan so close, not when she was still terrified of what would happen if he knew the truth. She couldn't let him in—not yet. The walls were still too high, the lies still too deep.

"I'm not ready," she whispered, her voice barely audible, more to herself than to him.

Ethan nodded slowly, his expression unreadable. "Whenever you are," he said softly. "I'll be here."

Vivienne watched him as he stood and walked away, the door chiming softly behind him as he left. She didn't know what had just happened, or what this connection between them meant, but for the first time, she felt a flicker of something in her chest—a sense of hope, of possibility.

But that hope was fragile. And as she sat there, her coffee now cold in front of her, she couldn't shake the feeling that the truth was coming for her. Sooner or later, the walls would come down, and she would have to face it. But the question was: would Ethan still be there when the truth was finally revealed?

Six

Growing Closer

The days that followed felt heavier than the last, a persistent sense of tension hanging over Vivienne like a storm cloud that refused to break. She couldn't escape the feeling that something was closing in around her, the walls of her carefully constructed life slowly crumbling under the weight of secrets she had worked so hard to bury. Ethan's words still echoed in her mind, and every time she saw him, every time they spoke, it was as if he could see right through her, peeling away the layers she had spent years building. She had to be careful. One wrong move, and everything she had worked for would be exposed.

But despite the lingering dread, there was also something else—a pull, an undeniable connection that had formed between her and Ethan. It wasn't just the curiosity he had sparked or the way he made her feel seen, for the first time, after so many years of hiding. There was a depth to their connection that went beyond words, beyond logic. It was something she couldn't explain, something that terrified her as much as it intrigued her.

As the week dragged on, Vivienne found herself walking the same paths she had taken since arriving in the town—through the quiet streets, along the shoreline, up to the small café where she had become a regular. She had come to crave the simplicity of it, the way the town moved at its own pace, unaffected by the frantic rush of the outside world. But as familiar as it had become, there was an underlying restlessness that gnawed at her, a sense that something was shifting beneath the surface.

One afternoon, as the sun dipped low in the sky, casting long shadows across the town, Vivienne made her way to the café, the cool breeze tugging at her hair. She hadn't seen Ethan since their last conversation, and though she tried to convince herself that it didn't matter, a part of her wondered if he would show up today. She couldn't deny that a small part of her longed to see him, to feel that connection again. But she couldn't allow herself to get too close. Not when the truth was still so far out of her reach.

When she entered the café, Alex was busy behind the counter, humming to himself as he prepared a fresh batch of pastries. The warmth of the room hit her like a comforting embrace, and for a moment, she allowed herself to relax, to forget about the weight of her thoughts. She ordered her usual, a cappuccino with just a touch of cinnamon, and made her way to the corner table by the window.

As she sipped her drink, her mind wandered. She found herself thinking about her family, about the life she had left behind. It felt like a lifetime ago, that version of herself—the ambitious young woman who had believed she could have it all. But now, with every passing day in this quiet town, she wondered if she had been chasing something that wasn't meant for her. She had come here hoping to find peace, to escape the suffocating weight of her past. But the longer she stayed, the more she realized that no matter how far she ran, her past would always be a part of her. And there was no running from that.

Lost in her thoughts, she didn't notice the figure that had entered the café until it was too late. The door chimed softly, and she looked up to see Ethan standing in the doorway. He glanced around the room, his eyes landing on her almost immediately. His presence seemed to fill the room, his confidence and ease drawing attention without effort.

Vivienne's heart skipped a beat. She quickly looked away, her fingers tightening around the handle of her coffee cup. She wasn't ready for this. She wasn't ready to face him again, not when her thoughts were still so tangled, not when the truth was threatening to spill out.

Ethan made his way to the counter, exchanging a few words with Alex, but his eyes kept flicking back to her. She could feel the weight of his gaze, even from across the room. And then, as if drawn by some invisible force, he began to walk toward her.

Vivienne's breath caught in her throat as he stopped at her table, standing in front of her with a slight, almost hesitant smile.

"Mind if I join you?" he asked, his voice calm but with an underlying edge that she couldn't quite place.

Vivienne hesitated, her mind racing. She could feel the walls closing in around her again, but she forced herself to meet his gaze. "I suppose you're already here," she said, her voice steady but with a faint trace of uncertainty.

Ethan sat down without waiting for an invitation, his eyes still searching hers, as if waiting for her to say something, anything. The silence stretched between them, heavy and pregnant with unspoken words. Vivienne felt her pulse quicken, the tension in the air palpable.

"I've been thinking about what you said," he finally spoke, his voice low and serious. "About you running from something. I don't want to push you, but I think I'm starting to understand what you're really hiding, Vera."

Vivienne's stomach dropped. She opened her mouth to speak, to deny it, to shut him down, but the words wouldn't come. Her heart was pounding now, each beat like a drum in her chest, echoing in her ears.

"I don't know what you mean," she said, forcing herself to sound confident, though inside, she was anything but.

Ethan leaned forward slightly, his eyes narrowing with a mixture of concern and curiosity. "You're not like the rest of the people here. You're not like the others who've come and gone. There's something about you, something you're not telling me."

Vivienne's hands trembled slightly, but she quickly steadied them, forcing her fingers to relax. She couldn't afford to show him any weakness. Not now, not when the stakes were so high.

"What are you trying to say?" she asked, trying to keep her voice neutral, but the undercurrent of fear was impossible to hide.

Ethan's gaze softened, but there was an intensity to it, as if he was seeing something in her that she couldn't see in herself. "I'm saying that you've been hiding in plain sight, Vera. You've built this life for yourself, but it's not real. It's a façade. You're running from something that's a part of you, something you can't outrun, no matter how far you go."

Vivienne felt the walls around her heart begin to crack, the pressure of the lie she had been living bearing down on her. She had worked so hard to keep it all hidden, to pretend that she was just like everyone else in this town. But Ethan was right. She was running. She was running from herself, from the truth, from the life that had been thrust upon her.

"I don't know what you want from me," she whispered, her voice trembling despite herself.

Ethan's expression softened, and for a moment, he didn't speak. He just watched her, his eyes filled with understanding, as if he could see the pain in her that she had spent so long hiding.

"I don't want anything from you, Vera," he said softly. "I just want you to stop running. Stop hiding. You don't have to do this alone."

The words hit her like a punch to the gut. She had spent so long convincing herself that she had to face everything alone, that no one could understand the weight of her past. But here was Ethan, offering her something she hadn't expected—an understanding, a connection that reached deeper than the lies she had told herself.

But as much as she wanted to believe him, to let herself be seen for who she truly was, fear still gripped her. The truth was a dangerous thing. It had the power to destroy everything she had built, everything she had worked so hard to protect.

"I can't," she whispered, the words barely audible. "You don't understand. You don't know what it's like…"

Ethan didn't press further. He just sat there, watching her with those quiet, knowing eyes. There was no judgment in his gaze, no impatience, just a steady presence that seemed to offer her some kind of peace, even if only for a moment.

"Whenever you're ready," he said, his voice gentle but firm. "I'll be here."

Vivienne looked away, unable to meet his gaze any longer. The weight of his words, the unspoken promise they held, threatened to break her. She wasn't ready. She couldn't be. But deep down, she knew that the time was coming when she would have to face the truth, when she would have to stop hiding.

For the first time since arriving in this town, Vivienne felt something shift inside her, a flicker of hope that maybe, just maybe, there was a way out of the shadows. But the road ahead was uncertain, and the cost of the truth was more than she was willing to pay.

Ethan stood up, his chair scraping softly against the floor. "I'll see you around, Vera," he said, his tone soft but filled with an understanding that left her breathless.

As he walked out of the café, the door chimed softly behind him, and Vivienne was left alone with the quiet hum of the room. She could feel the weight of everything pressing down on her—the truth, the lies, the connections she had made, and the ones she still feared.

And somewhere, deep inside, she knew that no matter how much she tried to avoid it, the rift between who she was and who she wanted to be was growing wider by the day. How much longer could she stay hidden in the shadows before the world, and Ethan, saw the truth?

Seven

The Truth Unveiled

The air in the café felt thicker than usual, as if the very walls themselves were closing in around Vivienne. The minutes stretched into hours, each one heavier than the last. She sat alone at the table where Ethan had just left, her fingers absently tracing the rim of her coffee cup, the bitter warmth of the drink doing little to quell the storm brewing inside her. She had told herself she was ready. Ready to leave the past behind, to let go of the life that had been forced upon her, and to live a life that was hers and hers alone. But as Ethan's words echoed in her mind, she realized just how far from ready she really was.

"I'm saying that you've been hiding in plain sight, Vera. You've built this life for yourself, but it's not real. It's a façade."

The words haunted her as the café grew busier around her.

In the Shadows of Her Fortune

She had always prided herself on her ability to control her emotions, to hide behind the carefully constructed layers of her new identity. But with each passing moment, those layers seemed to crack. The walls she had so carefully built around her heart were starting to crumble, and with them, the version of herself she had come to rely on.

She couldn't shake the feeling that she was being pulled in two directions. The quiet life she had imagined here, in this small town, where no one knew her, where no one expected anything from her, seemed so far out of reach now. And then there was the part of her that knew, deep down, that she couldn't keep running forever. Sooner or later, the truth would catch up with her, and when it did, it would change everything.

Her thoughts were interrupted by the sudden ring of her phone, the sound sharp in the otherwise quiet room. Vivienne glanced at the screen, the name flashing across it sending a chill through her.

Mother.

Vivienne let the phone ring for a moment, her heart beating faster in her chest. She had been dreading this. The moment she knew would come, when her family would start to notice her absence, when her mother would track her down and demand answers. She had hoped, in some foolish part of her heart, that she could escape them. But deep down, she knew that wasn't possible. No matter how far she ran, they would always find her.

The Truth Unveiled

The phone stopped ringing before Vivienne could gather the strength to answer it. She exhaled sharply, a mix of relief and dread flooding her chest. She wasn't ready to face them—not yet, not while the life she had built for herself here was still so fragile.

But as she sat there, staring at the empty space in front of her, she couldn't help but wonder how much longer she could hold on to the illusion of a new life. Her mother was persistent, her family relentless. And no matter how much she tried to convince herself that she was free, the truth always seemed to hover just out of reach, waiting for the moment when it would drag her back into the world she had desperately tried to escape.

Vivienne picked up her phone, her fingers trembling slightly as she opened the message from her mother.

"Vivienne, I know you're avoiding my calls. Don't think I don't know where you are. I'll give you until the end of the week to come home. If you don't, I'll send someone to find you."

Vivienne's heart pounded in her chest. Her mother was never one for subtlety. There was no negotiating, no compromise. She was the head of the Hart family, a woman who ruled her empire with an iron fist. Vivienne had never been able to escape that. No matter how far she ran, her family's influence was always just behind her, pulling her back into the fold.

She stared at the screen for a long moment, the words on it blurring as her mind raced. Her mother had given her an ultimatum. She had made it clear that there was no choice in the matter—either she came home and took her place as the heir to the Hart fortune, or she would be dragged back into it kicking and screaming. Vivienne felt the weight of that decision settle over her like a cold shadow.

She had to choose.

But how could she choose when the very thing that had driven her to leave—her family, her inheritance, the life they had mapped out for her—was the one thing she couldn't seem to escape?

She felt a hand on her shoulder, the warmth of it startling against the cold emptiness she had been holding inside for so long. Vivienne turned to find Ethan standing behind her, his eyes soft, his expression unreadable. He had come back.

"I didn't mean to interrupt," he said quietly, his voice low but steady. "But I thought you might need a little distraction."

Vivienne looked at him, unsure of what to say. The pull between them was undeniable, but she couldn't let herself be distracted by it. Not now. Not when the truth was so close to breaking through. She had to keep her focus, had to stay in control.

"I—I appreciate it," she said, her voice softer than she intended. "But I have a lot on my mind."

Ethan nodded, his gaze steady, but there was something in his eyes that made her want to tell him everything. To let go of the lie, to stop pretending that she could keep running forever.

The Truth Unveiled

But she couldn't do that—not yet. Not until she had made her choice.

"You don't have to face this alone," he said, as if reading her thoughts. "Whatever it is, I'm here. You don't have to carry it all by yourself."

His words hit her like a tidal wave, crashing over the carefully constructed walls she had built. She wanted to believe him. She wanted to believe that there was someone who would stand by her, someone who would understand. But the truth was, she had never let anyone in before. She had never allowed herself to rely on anyone but herself. And now, when the stakes were so high, it felt too dangerous to let go.

"Thank you," she whispered, her voice barely audible. She looked away, trying to hide the fear in her eyes. "But this is something I have to do on my own."

Ethan didn't argue. He simply nodded, his eyes lingering on her for a moment longer before he turned to leave. But as he reached the door, he paused, glancing back over his shoulder.

"Whenever you're ready, Vera," he said softly. "I'll be here."

And just like that, he was gone, leaving Vivienne alone with the weight of her decision. Alone with the truth that she couldn't escape, no matter how hard she tried.

The café was quieter now, the hum of conversation fading into the background as Vivienne sat in the silence of her own thoughts. The words from her mother echoed in her mind, and the weight of the decision before her felt heavier than ever.

She couldn't keep running. She had already made that choice. But what came next? Was she ready to face the life she had left behind, to face the truth of who she really was? Or was she destined to fall back into the world she had tried so desperately to escape?

The phone in her hand vibrated again, and she glanced down to see a new message from her mother.

"You have until tomorrow, Vivienne. You can't hide forever."

Vivienne swallowed hard, the lump in her throat making it difficult to breathe. Tomorrow. She had one more day. One more day to decide between the life she had chosen and the life that had been thrust upon her. One more day before the rift between who she was and who she was meant to be would finally tear apart.

She stood up, her legs unsteady beneath her, and walked to the door, the cold air of the evening hitting her like a shock to the system. The world seemed to stretch out before her, a vast expanse of choices, of consequences, of unknowns. And somewhere in the distance, she knew that when she took that first step, she would either fall through reality or find a way to hold onto it.

But for now, she was standing at the edge, waiting for the inevitable.

Eight

The Conflict of Worlds

Vivienne sat on the edge of her bed, staring out the window at the darkened town below. The streetlights cast long, flickering shadows across the empty roads, and the quiet hum of the night felt almost suffocating. The weight of the decision pressing on her chest was unbearable. Tomorrow, everything would change. She would either face the reality of her past or continue running from it, hiding in the small town she had come to think of as a sanctuary.

Her phone sat on the nightstand, silent but ever-present. Her mother's message from earlier that day still lingered in her mind, the words burning into her thoughts like a brand. You can't hide forever.

The truth was, Vivienne wasn't sure if she wanted to hide anymore. For so long, she had convinced herself that the only way to escape the suffocating life she had been born into was to leave it behind completely. She had created a new identity, a new life, and for a brief time, it had felt real. She had felt free. But that freedom had been short-lived. Every conversation with Ethan, every moment of connection, only reminded her of the truth she had been running from: no matter how far she went, she could never truly escape who she was.

Her hand rested on the cold glass of the window, her fingertips brushing lightly against it as though trying to touch the stars above. She had made her choices, but she wasn't ready to face them.

The knock on the door was soft, but it was enough to pull Vivienne from her thoughts. Her heart skipped a beat as she glanced at the door. Who would be knocking at this hour? She had expected the night to pass in solitude, with only her thoughts and the weight of her decision to keep her company.

The knock came again, firmer this time, as if the person on the other side was growing impatient. Vivienne stood up slowly, a sense of unease rising in her chest. She knew who it was. She didn't have to ask. She had felt it in the air the moment she had allowed herself to admit that she was being pulled toward Ethan, that the connection between them was more than just a passing encounter.

She opened the door, and Ethan stood there, silhouetted by the soft light from the hallway behind him. His figure was tall and commanding, yet there was something gentle in his posture, something that made her heart beat faster.

"I thought I might find you here," he said softly, his voice low and calm.

Vivienne didn't say anything at first. She just stood there, watching him, her heart racing in her chest. He had always been so composed, so sure of himself, but now she could see the uncertainty in his eyes. It mirrored the turmoil inside her—the battle between the life she had built and the one she was being called back to.

"I wasn't expecting you," she said, her voice barely above a whisper. The words sounded hollow, but she couldn't help them. She didn't want him to see the confusion, the fear, that she was trying so hard to hide.

Ethan stepped into the room, closing the door gently behind him. His eyes searched hers, studying her face as if trying to understand what was happening inside her mind. He didn't need to ask the questions she was avoiding. He knew. She had been running for so long, and now it seemed like the chase was finally catching up with her.

"You've been avoiding me," he said quietly, the words cutting through the tension in the room. "And I don't blame you. I've seen the way you've been pushing me away, the walls you've put up."

Vivienne swallowed, the lump in her throat making it hard to breathe. She had never wanted to be vulnerable, never wanted to admit that she was struggling, that she didn't know how to face the truth. But Ethan had always been different. There was something about him—something she couldn't explain—that made her want to let him in, made her want to trust him with everything she had been hiding.

"I didn't want to drag you into this," she whispered, her voice shaking slightly. "I didn't want anyone to see the mess I've made of my life."

Ethan stepped closer to her, his hand gently cupping her cheek. His touch was warm, grounding, and for the first time in weeks, Vivienne felt like she wasn't alone. The weight of her fears, of the choices she had made, didn't feel so heavy when he was near.

"You don't have to carry this alone, Vivienne," Ethan said softly, his thumb brushing over her skin as if to reassure her. "I don't want to force you to share everything you're carrying, but I want you to know that I'm here. Whatever you're running from, whatever you're afraid of, you don't have to face it by yourself."

Vivienne closed her eyes, leaning into his touch, the vulnerability threatening to break her down. She had never let anyone get this close before, never allowed someone to see her weaknesses, to see her fear. But Ethan wasn't just anyone. He had become something more, someone who saw beyond the surface, someone who could sense the parts of her that she was too afraid to acknowledge.

"You don't understand," she whispered, her voice barely audible. "My family... they won't let me go. I've tried to leave them behind, but they keep pulling me back in. They've built a life for me that I never asked for, and I don't know how to escape it. I don't know how to be free."

Ethan's hand moved from her cheek to her shoulder, his fingers gently squeezing in an effort to comfort her. He didn't speak right away, instead allowing the silence between them to fill the room with a sense of understanding. He wasn't judging her. He wasn't trying to fix things. He was just there—present, unwavering, and patient.

"I know what it's like," he said finally, his voice low and sincere. "I know what it's like to feel like your life is being controlled by others. To feel like you're being pulled in directions you never asked for. But that doesn't have to be your reality. You're not stuck, Vivienne. You have a choice."

Vivienne looked up at him, her heart pounding in her chest. For the first time, she wasn't sure if she could make that choice. She had spent so long running from the life her family had designed for her, running from the expectations they had placed on her shoulders, that she wasn't sure who she would be without that weight. But there was a part of her, a small, quiet part, that was beginning to believe that maybe she could let go. Maybe she could choose herself for the first time in her life.

"I'm scared," she confessed, her voice trembling. "I don't know what will happen if I let go. If I walk away from everything I've known, from everything they've made me believe about myself... I don't know who I'll be."

Ethan didn't hesitate. His hand gently cupped her face, his thumb brushing across her cheek in a soothing gesture. "You'll be you, Vivienne. The real you. The one who isn't weighed down by the past or by other people's expectations. You don't have to let them define who you are. You don't have to let them decide your future."

His words resonated deep inside her, stirring something she had long buried. The idea of freedom, the idea of walking away from everything that had defined her, was terrifying. But there was also something intoxicating about it. The idea that she could finally be free—to make her own choices, to define her own life, and to find her own happiness—was a thought she hadn't allowed herself to entertain in years.

"I don't know if I'm strong enough to do it," Vivienne admitted, her voice barely above a whisper.

Ethan smiled softly, his eyes filled with warmth and tenderness. "You are. I know you are."

For a long moment, they simply stood there, the weight of the world pressing down on them. Vivienne could feel the pull between them, the connection that had been growing ever since they first met. It was more than just chemistry or attraction. It was something deeper, something that transcended time and circumstance. And in that moment, she knew that Ethan was more than just a distraction. He was a part of her future. He was the one person who had managed to see beyond the façade she had built around herself.

She reached up, her hand trembling slightly as it touched his chest, feeling the steady beat of his heart beneath her fingertips. For the first time in a long time, Vivienne felt something that had been missing from her life for so long: hope.

"I don't want to lose you," she whispered, her voice barely audible.

Ethan looked down at her, his eyes filled with understanding. "You won't," he said softly. "You never will. But you have to choose. You have to choose yourself first."

Vivienne closed her eyes, taking a deep breath. Tomorrow would come, and with it, the choice she had been avoiding for so long. She didn't know what the future held, but for the first time, she wasn't afraid to face it. She wasn't afraid to take that step, to fall through reality and embrace the life she had always wanted.

With Ethan by her side, she knew that she could face whatever came next.

Nine

A Test of Love

The morning light filtered through the thin curtains of Vivienne's small room, casting a muted glow over the bare walls. The town outside was still wrapped in the quiet calm of the early hours, the streets empty except for the occasional car rolling by. The world was still, waiting. But Vivienne was anything but still.

She sat on the edge of the bed, her fingers nervously twisting the corner of the blanket. Her thoughts were scattered, caught between the reality she had left behind and the uncertain future that awaited her. Ethan's words from the night before echoed in her mind, the truth they held lingering like a weight she couldn't escape. *You don't have to let them define who you are. You don't have to let them decide your future.*

But as much as she wanted to believe him, as much as part of her longed for freedom, the thought of facing her family again, of confronting the past she had spent so long running from, felt like an insurmountable mountain. Could she really break free from the chains of her inheritance? Could she defy the expectations that had been placed on her since birth?

A sharp knock at the door broke her from her spiraling thoughts. Vivienne's heart leaped in her chest, her breath catching in her throat. She hadn't expected anyone, not this early, not when her decision was still in the balance.

"Vivienne?" came a voice from the other side of the door, soft but insistent. It was Alex, the café owner, his voice tinged with concern. "You alright in there?"

Vivienne stood up quickly, smoothing out her clothes as she moved toward the door. She didn't want to talk about what was going through her mind right now, didn't want to admit to anyone that she was standing at the edge of a precipice, unsure of whether she would fall or fly.

"I'm fine, Alex," she said, her voice steady despite the storm inside her. "Just thinking."

Alex hesitated for a moment before speaking again. "I know I'm not the one you've been talking to, but if you need someone, I'm here. I've been through a lot myself, and sometimes it helps to share the burden."

Vivienne's throat tightened, the sincerity in Alex's voice pulling at something deep inside her. She appreciated the offer, truly, but she couldn't share her burden with anyone. Not now. Not with so much at stake.

"I know," she said softly, her hand resting on the doorknob. "Thank you, really. I just need some time."

With a final nod, Alex's footsteps retreated down the hallway, leaving Vivienne alone once more. She closed her eyes, letting out a shaky breath, trying to steady herself. The decision she had to make was still there, looming large. She couldn't put it off any longer. But how could she make the right choice when both paths seemed to lead to different versions of herself?

She moved to the window, pulling the curtains open just a fraction. The sun was beginning to rise higher in the sky, the warmth of it slowly stretching across the town. She could feel the pull of it, the call to step outside, to embrace the unknown. But what would it cost her? Could she really leave behind the life she had been born into, the expectations of her family, the wealth and power that had defined her existence?

And then there was Ethan.

Her heart stuttered at the thought of him. After everything they had shared, after all the moments of connection, he had become more than just a passing acquaintance. He had become a tether, a connection to a life she wasn't sure she was ready for. She hadn't allowed herself to acknowledge it fully, but the truth was undeniable: Ethan had come to mean more to her than she could have ever imagined. He had shown her a glimpse of a different world, one where she could be free, where she could choose for herself, without the weight of her family's expectations hanging over her every move.

But what if she chose him? What would that mean for her? Would she be betraying everything she had worked for, everything her family had worked for? And what if he wasn't the person she thought he was? What if, like everyone else, he only wanted a part of her—only wanted the illusion of freedom without truly understanding the consequences?

She closed her eyes again, the questions swirling in her mind like a tornado. *How could I live with myself if I walk away from my family? How could I ever forgive myself?*

The sound of the café door swinging open interrupted her thoughts. She knew without turning around that it was Ethan. There was a quiet certainty in the way he moved, a calmness that had always drawn her to him.

"Vera," he said softly, his voice a whisper in the stillness of the room. "Can we talk?"

Vivienne turned slowly, her heart already beating faster in her chest. He stood at the threshold of the room, his hands shoved into his pockets, his gaze steady but full of an emotion she couldn't quite place.

She nodded, her throat dry. "I've been waiting for you."

Ethan's lips quirked upward in a small, knowing smile. He took a step closer, but there was something different in his demeanor now—something guarded, as if he too understood that this conversation was more than just about them. It was about everything that had been building between them, the tangled threads that had woven their lives together without either of them fully realizing it.

"I know you've been avoiding me," he said quietly. "I can see it in the way you look at me, the way you pull away. I don't know what's going on inside your head, Vivienne, but I can't stand by and watch you push me away when I know that there's something between us. Something real."

Vivienne's chest tightened at his words, the truth in them ringing louder than anything she had ever heard before. It was impossible to deny it now. The connection was there, undeniable. But there was still so much she couldn't share, so much that was locked inside her.

"I'm not running from you," she said, her voice barely a whisper. "I'm running from myself."

Ethan stepped closer, his eyes soft but intense. "You don't have to run from yourself. You're stronger than you think, Vivienne. You've been running your whole life, but it's time to face what's waiting for you. Whatever that is."

She swallowed hard, her hands trembling as she reached up to touch his arm. The sensation of his skin beneath her fingertips was grounding, a reminder that there was still something real between them, something worth fighting for. But the weight of her decision was too much to bear alone.

"I don't know who I am anymore," she admitted, her voice breaking. "I don't know what to do."

Ethan's hand gently cupped her face, his thumb brushing over her cheek in a comforting gesture. "You know who you are, Vivienne. You just have to stop letting everyone else tell you who you should be. The choice is yours. You've always had the power to make it, but you've been too afraid to claim it."

The words sank deep into her soul, their weight pressing down on her. Could she really do it? Could she really take control of her life, choose who she was meant to be, and walk away from everything that had defined her? Or would she always be tethered to her family, to the legacy they had created for her?

Vivienne closed her eyes, trying to steady her breathing, trying to ignore the fear that was clawing its way up from the pit of her stomach. She could feel the ground shifting beneath her, the very foundation of her existence crumbling with every passing second. There was no going back now.

"Tell me what to do," she whispered, her voice hoarse. "I don't know if I can do this alone."

Ethan's hand dropped from her face, and for a moment, he said nothing. He just stood there, watching her, as though waiting for her to make the choice herself. His silence wasn't uncomfortable—it was reassuring. He wasn't asking her to make a decision now, but he was offering her the space to come to her own conclusions.

"You're not alone, Vivienne," he said, his voice steady. "You've never been alone. Not while I'm here."

And with that, everything inside her shifted. The fear, the confusion, the self-doubt—it all melted away. For the first time in a long time, Vivienne felt like she could breathe again. She didn't have all the answers, and she didn't know what the future would hold, but she knew one thing: whatever came next, she wasn't facing it alone.

"Then let's go," she said, her voice stronger now, filled with a newfound resolve. "Let's take the first step together."

Ethan's smile was gentle, but his eyes were filled with something deeper—something that told her, without words, that no matter what happened, they would face it together. The uncertainty, the fear, the past—all of it was still there, but it no longer controlled her.

She was ready. Finally, she was ready. And with Ethan by her side, she knew that whatever happened next, they would find a way through it.

Ten

The Burden of Wealth

The crisp morning air bit at Vivienne's skin as she stepped out of the cottage, the sun barely peeking over the horizon. The town was still quiet, the streets deserted as she made her way toward the café. Every step felt like a step into the unknown. Her heart pounded in her chest as the weight of her decision settled over her. She had told Ethan the truth. She had admitted the fear that had been holding her back all this time—the fear of her past, the fear of facing her family, the fear of losing herself in a life she never chose. But now, she was free of that fear. She had taken the first step toward the future, toward a life that was truly hers.

As she walked, her thoughts drifted back to that first day she had arrived in this town. She had been running then, searching for something—anything—that could offer her a reprieve from the life she had left behind. She hadn't known then what she was looking for. But now, as the town slowly woke up around her, she realized that she had found something—someone—that made her feel like she could finally stop running.

Ethan.

Her heart skipped at the thought of him. She had never expected him to be the one to pull her from the darkness, to help her face the truth of who she was. He had been patient, steady, never pushing her too hard, but always there, watching, waiting for her to see what she hadn't yet been able to see in herself. He had offered her more than just love. He had offered her a chance at a new life. And now, for the first time in years, Vivienne felt like she could finally breathe.

She reached the café, the familiar scent of freshly brewed coffee filling the air. The door creaked as she pushed it open, stepping inside. The warmth of the room enveloped her, a sharp contrast to the chill of the morning air. She looked around, but Ethan wasn't there yet. The soft murmur of conversation and the clinking of coffee cups were the only sounds in the room.

Vivienne moved to her usual table by the window, her mind swirling with thoughts of what was to come. She couldn't stay hidden in the shadows forever. Her mother's ultimatum still lingered in the back of her mind. She had to decide—now. But for the first time in a long time, she felt like she had the power to choose.

As she sat down, her phone buzzed in her pocket. Vivienne's heart skipped. She pulled it out, seeing a message from Ethan.

I'll be there soon. Let's talk.

The simplicity of his words sent a rush of warmth through her chest. There was no pretense, no pressure—just the invitation to face whatever came next, together. She smiled, feeling a sense of calm settle over her. She wasn't alone. Not anymore.

Her fingers absently traced the edge of the coffee cup in front of her as she waited. She thought of the decision she had to make—of the life she had chosen to leave behind, and the life that awaited her. She could feel the weight of it, pressing on her chest, suffocating in its intensity. It was a choice between the world she had been born into and the one she could finally build for herself. There was no easy answer. But for the first time, she didn't feel like she was drowning in the decision. For the first time, she felt like she had control.

Her thoughts were interrupted by the sound of the door opening. She looked up to see Ethan step inside, his familiar, easy smile lighting up his face as he scanned the room. When his eyes met hers, a flicker of something passed between them, something deep and unspoken. She felt it in the pit of her stomach, the connection that had grown between them over the past few weeks. He was here. He had kept his promise. And for the first time in her life, Vivienne felt like she wasn't the only one making this journey.

Ethan made his way toward her, his presence filling the space between them like a magnet. When he reached her, he slid into the seat across from her, his eyes still soft, but with a new intensity that made Vivienne's heart race.

"Morning," he said, his voice warm and steady, like the first rays of sunlight breaking through the darkness.

"Morning," she replied, her voice a little shaky, but she couldn't help the smile that tugged at her lips. She wanted to tell him everything—the fear, the doubts, the weight of the decision she had been carrying—but right now, with him sitting across from her, she didn't need to say a word. He understood.

Ethan's smile softened, and he reached across the table, his hand brushing lightly against hers. The simple touch sent a shiver down her spine. "Are you ready?" he asked, his voice quiet but filled with a kind of certainty that made her believe in herself, even when she wasn't sure she could.

Vivienne's breath caught in her throat. The moment had come. The moment she had been avoiding, the moment she had been dreading. The choice was in her hands now. She looked down at their hands, her fingers curling around his, and felt a calmness settle over her. She had been running for so long, but now, as she stared at Ethan, she realized that she didn't have to run anymore.

"I don't know if I'm ready," she admitted, her voice barely a whisper. "But I know I have to choose."

Ethan didn't say anything at first. He just watched her, his gaze steady, his expression open. The silence between them wasn't uncomfortable—it was the kind of silence that spoke volumes, the kind that only two people who truly understood each other could share.

"You've already made the choice, Vivienne," Ethan said softly. "You just don't know it yet."

Vivienne's heart skipped a beat. She opened her mouth to respond, but the words died on her lips. She realized, in that moment, that Ethan was right. The choice had already been made. She had been fighting it, denying it, but deep down, she had known all along. The life she had been living wasn't real. It had been a construct, a façade to protect herself from the truth. But now, the truth was staring her in the face.

She had chosen this life. She had chosen Ethan. She had chosen herself.

A wave of emotion hit her, and for the first time in a long time, Vivienne felt a sense of peace wash over her. The uncertainty, the fear, the doubts—they didn't matter anymore. She wasn't alone. She didn't have to face the future on her own. With Ethan by her side, she could finally be free.

"I'm ready," she said finally, her voice strong, filled with a newfound conviction. "I'm ready to face whatever comes next."

Ethan's smile widened, and for a moment, it felt like the world around them disappeared. There was no past, no future—there was only this moment, this choice, and the promise of something real.

"I knew you were," he said softly, his thumb brushing over the back of her hand. "And I'll be with you every step of the way."

Vivienne squeezed his hand, the warmth of his touch grounding her in a way nothing else could. She could feel the world shifting beneath her, the path ahead opening up, and for the first time, she wasn't afraid of what it held.

Together, they would face the unknown. Together, they would build a future that was theirs. And with Ethan by her side, Vivienne knew that whatever happened, they would be ready.

Eleven

A Chance Encounter

Vivienne stepped out of the café, the cool breeze of the early evening air brushing against her skin. The sky above had faded into hues of deep orange and purple, the last traces of daylight slowly succumbing to the darkening night. But even the beauty of the sunset couldn't ease the gnawing tension building in her chest. The decision had been made. She had chosen. She had taken the first step toward freedom, toward a life that was finally hers to control.

But as she walked through the quiet streets, her thoughts remained clouded, caught between the weight of her past and the uncertainty of her future. She had chosen Ethan. She had chosen herself. But what did that really mean? What would her family think? Her mother's ultimatum still lingered in the back of her mind, a constant reminder that she couldn't hide forever. The clock was ticking, and the moment when she would have to face her family's demands was drawing closer.

She could feel the rift growing, a chasm between the life she had been born into and the life she was desperately trying to build for herself. She had always known that the two worlds could never truly coexist, but now, with each passing day, the divide felt wider, more unbridgeable. There was no going back, no way to return to the life she had once known.

As Vivienne continued her walk, her thoughts consumed by the future, a familiar voice called out to her from behind.

"Vera!"

She turned around, her heart skipping a beat as she saw Alex jogging toward her. He was breathless, his face flushed from running, but there was a sense of urgency in his eyes that made her stomach twist.

"What's wrong?" she asked, her heart racing. Alex had always been easygoing, never the type to seem worried about anything. But tonight, something was different.

Alex reached her, his chest heaving as he tried to catch his breath. "I—" He paused for a moment, clearly gathering his thoughts. "I need to talk to you. It's about Ethan."

Vivienne's stomach dropped. She didn't need to hear more. She had felt it all along—the unease that had been building between her and Ethan. She had known, deep down, that their connection, as real as it felt, couldn't possibly be as simple as it seemed. There was always something more, something she hadn't been able to see. And now, the weight of that uncertainty pressed down on her like a lead weight.

"What about Ethan?" she asked, her voice suddenly sharp. She couldn't mask the anxiety rising inside her, the fear of what Alex might say.

"It's not what you think," Alex replied quickly, his voice filled with urgency. "It's just—there are things you don't know. Things about him. Things that I'm not sure you're ready to hear."

Vivienne's breath caught in her throat. Her mind raced, every possible scenario flashing before her eyes. She had spent so much time trying to avoid the past, trying to bury the parts of her life she didn't want to face, that she hadn't taken the time to truly understand what was happening between her and Ethan. Was this another illusion, another mistake? Was she simply running toward something that didn't exist?

"Tell me," she demanded, her voice strained. "What do you mean? What things?"

Alex hesitated for a long moment, his eyes darting around the street as though he were looking for someone—or something—that wasn't there. When he finally spoke, his voice was low, barely a whisper.

"I don't know how to explain it," Alex said, his eyes locking with hers. "But Ethan's not who he says he is. He's not just some guy you met here. He's... he's connected to everything. To your family. To the life you thought you left behind."

Vivienne felt her world shift on its axis. The ground beneath her feet seemed to tremble, the streetlights flickering in her peripheral vision as if the very fabric of reality had been stretched too thin. The words didn't make sense. They couldn't. Ethan wasn't involved in her family's business. He couldn't be. He couldn't be a part of the world she had run from.

But the look on Alex's face told a different story. There was no mistaking the seriousness in his eyes. He wasn't joking. He wasn't playing games.

"What are you saying?" Vivienne asked, her voice trembling despite her best efforts to remain calm. "Are you telling me Ethan's been lying to me?"

Alex shook his head, his gaze sympathetic but filled with an edge of fear. "It's not that simple. It's not just lies. There's more to him than you realize. More than he's let on."

Vivienne's heart pounded in her chest. She couldn't breathe. Her thoughts were a blur, confusion and disbelief racing through her mind. She had felt the connection between them—how could it have been anything other than real? How could she have been so blind?

"Alex, you're not making any sense," she said, her voice barely above a whisper. "What are you talking about? Ethan isn't part of my world. He's just a—"

A Chance Encounter

"A distraction?" Alex finished for her, his words sharp. "That's what you think? Do you really think he's just some ordinary guy? That he's not involved in all of this somehow?"

Vivienne stared at him, her mind reeling. Ethan was the one person she had let herself trust. He was the one person who had made her feel like she wasn't alone, like she could finally escape the life she had been born into. And now, Alex was telling her that everything she had believed about him was a lie?

"Tell me what you know," Vivienne demanded, her voice steady despite the storm brewing inside her. "Tell me everything."

Alex hesitated again, looking down at the ground, his hands clenched into fists at his sides. "I don't have all the answers. But I've seen things, Vivienne. Things that don't add up. Ethan's been doing things, asking questions about your family, about your father's business, and I've seen him talking to people who aren't exactly... on the up and up. He's got connections you don't know about. And they're dangerous."

Vivienne felt her chest tighten, the breath caught in her throat. The fear was back, but this time, it wasn't just fear for herself. It was fear for Ethan. Fear that everything she thought she knew about him—everything she had come to trust—was a carefully constructed lie.

"What are you saying?" she asked again, her voice barely audible.

"I don't know everything," Alex said, his voice cracking with the weight of his own uncertainty. "But I'm telling you, Vivienne, you need to be careful. Ethan's not just some guy you fell for. He's got a past, a dangerous one. And I'm not sure you're ready for what you might find out."

The words echoed in her mind like a broken record. Dangerous. Past. Connections. Vivienne felt a cold sweat break out on her skin as the world around her seemed to tilt. The town, the life she had been building here, felt like it was slipping away, unraveling in real-time. The pull of her family, the life she had left behind, the choices she had made—everything was collapsing into one chaotic, overwhelming mess.

"I don't believe you," Vivienne whispered, the words coming out as a desperate plea. "Ethan wouldn't do that. He wouldn't lie to me."

Alex's expression softened, but his eyes were filled with a deep sorrow that Vivienne couldn't ignore. "I'm not saying he's the villain here. But there's something bigger going on, Vivienne. And you're in the middle of it. You've always been in the middle of it."

The weight of his words hit her like a physical blow. She had always known there was more to her life, more to her family's legacy than she wanted to admit. But this? This was something she wasn't ready to face. The world she had tried to leave behind was reaching back for her, pulling her in, dragging her toward something far more dangerous than she could have ever imagined.

"I have to go," Vivienne said, her voice shaking as she turned and started walking away. She didn't know where she was going, but she needed space, time to think, time to make sense of everything Alex had said.

"Vivienne!" Alex called after her, but she didn't stop. She couldn't stop.

Her mind was spinning, every step she took feeling like a step further away from everything she had tried to build. Ethan. Her family. The life she had known. They were all connected in ways she didn't yet understand, ways that were darker than she could have ever imagined.

The town, the quiet streets, everything she had once found comfort in, now felt like a trap, and she was caught in the middle of it all. How much of what she had built here was real? How much of it was part of the game her family had been playing all along?

And just as she thought she couldn't bear it anymore, a hand grabbed her arm, pulling her sharply to a stop. She turned around, her heart racing, to find Ethan standing there, his eyes wide with concern.

"I was coming to find you," he said, his voice hoarse, almost desperate. "We need to talk."

And in that moment, Vivienne knew that the truth was coming for her.

Twelve

Rebuilding Trust

Vivienne's heart raced as Ethan's hand gripped her arm, pulling her to a stop in the middle of the narrow, deserted street. She could feel the pulse of her own blood rushing in her ears, drowning out the steady rhythm of the world around them. It was as though everything had gone still—frozen in time, hanging on the precipice of something far bigger than her.

The weight of the past few days crushed down on her shoulders, the tension from Alex's cryptic warning clinging to her like a second skin. Every word he had said reverberated through her mind: Ethan's not who you think he is. He's not just some guy you met here. He's connected to everything.

It didn't make sense. She refused to believe it. Ethan wasn't like that. He couldn't be. But now, standing here in the dim light of the evening, a part of her wondered if the pull between them had been nothing more than a mirage—an illusion she had desperately wanted to be true.

"I wasn't expecting this," Vivienne said, her voice tight, fighting to suppress the anxiety gnawing at her. She jerked her arm free from his grasp, her movements jerky and unsteady. "I need answers, Ethan. I need to understand what's going on."

Ethan stepped back, his face hardening. His expression shifted from the concern she had grown accustomed to, to something guarded, something she didn't fully recognize. He glanced around, as if making sure no one else was nearby. The silence between them felt thick, almost suffocating.

"I told you," he said finally, his voice low and even. "We need to talk. This can't wait any longer."

Vivienne's heart hammered in her chest, the knot of unease tightening with each passing second. She had been running from her past for so long, hiding from the people and the legacy that had shaped her life. But now, the past was catching up to her, closing in like a predator waiting to strike. And the one person she had trusted the most, the one person who had pulled her from the darkness, was standing right in front of her—holding pieces of a truth she wasn't ready to face.

"I don't want your secrets, Ethan," she said, her voice trembling despite her best efforts to remain steady. "I don't want to find out that everything between us has been a lie. If you're part of the life I've been running from, then you should have just stayed away."

Ethan's face flinched, as though her words cut deeper than she had intended. He stepped forward, closing the distance between them, his eyes searching hers as though he was trying to find some trace of understanding, some flicker of trust that had once been there. But Vivienne felt herself retreating into the fortress she had built around her heart.

"I never wanted this, Vivienne," Ethan said softly, his voice carrying a rawness she hadn't heard before. "I never wanted you to find out like this. But it's not just about you or me. It's bigger than that. It's about everything. Your family. The people who've been pulling the strings behind the scenes. And I... I'm tangled in the middle of it."

Vivienne froze. His words hit her like a tidal wave, crashing over her with such force that she struggled to catch her breath. Her legs felt weak, the world tilting beneath her as she tried to piece together what he was saying.

"What do you mean?" she whispered, her voice barely audible.

Ethan ran a hand through his hair, his expression hardening once again. "There are things you don't know, things about your family's business, about the legacy they've built. I've been involved for years, but I never meant for you to get caught up in it. I didn't want you to be dragged into the mess that is my past."

Vivienne's pulse quickened, her mind racing. Everything she

thought she understood about Ethan—the connection they had, the love they had built—was beginning to unravel before her eyes. She had trusted him. She had opened up to him in ways she hadn't done with anyone else. And now, he was telling her that everything was a lie, that he had been hiding something from her, something that tied him to her family in ways she couldn't comprehend.

"Why didn't you tell me?" Vivienne asked, her voice tight, the bitterness of betrayal beginning to rise in her throat. "Why didn't you trust me?"

"I did trust you," Ethan said, his voice raw. "But there were things I couldn't explain. I couldn't drag you into it, Vivienne. You were already running from your family. The last thing I wanted to do was make you feel trapped again. But it's too late now. I've dragged you into it whether I wanted to or not. And now, you have to make a choice."

Vivienne's eyes burned with unshed tears as she struggled to make sense of everything. She had spent so long trying to escape the legacy of her family, the chains that bound her to a past she didn't want. And now, it was all coming back. She was stuck between two worlds—the one she had left behind and the one she was trying to build. But Ethan... Ethan had been part of both.

Her voice shook as she spoke again, the words spilling out like a dam breaking. "What do you want from me, Ethan? What are you asking me to do?"

"I'm asking you to choose," he said, his eyes darkening with a mixture of regret and resolve. "You can walk away. You can leave all of this behind and go back to the life you had before. But if you do that, you'll never be free. You'll always be tied to them, to your family's expectations. Or…" His voice faltered for a moment, before he met her gaze again, his expression hardening with determination. "Or you can fight for something real. You can fight for a life of your own. With me. But it won't be easy. There's no going back once you make that choice."

Vivienne's chest tightened as his words sank in. A life of her own? What did that even mean? Everything she had ever known was tied to her family, to their expectations, to the wealth and power they had given her. And now, Ethan was offering her a way out—but it wasn't as simple as walking away. It wasn't as easy as choosing him. It was a fight, a battle against everything she had been raised to believe. And she wasn't sure if she was strong enough to face it.

"I don't know if I can do this," Vivienne whispered, her voice trembling with fear and uncertainty. "I don't know if I can be the person you want me to be. The person I want to be. My family… they're everything. They control everything. How can I just walk away from all of that?"

Ethan stepped closer to her, his hand gently cupping her face, as though trying to pull her back from the edge. "You're stronger than you think, Vivienne. You've been running from this for so long because you think it defines you. But it doesn't. You're not your family's legacy. You're not the sum of their expectations. You're more than that. And I believe in you. I believe in us."

Rebuilding Trust

Tears welled up in Vivienne's eyes, the rawness of his words breaking down the walls she had so carefully constructed. For the first time, she didn't feel like she was alone in this fight. For the first time, she felt like she had someone who believed in her, someone who was willing to stand beside her, no matter what came next.

But the choice wasn't easy. She couldn't simply walk away from her family's power and wealth without consequence. She couldn't just step into the life Ethan was offering without facing the storm that would follow. The world she had known was a tangled mess of lies and expectations. And no matter what she chose, it would never be the same again.

"I'm scared, Ethan," Vivienne said softly, her voice breaking. "I don't know if I can do this."

Ethan pulled her into his arms, holding her close, his breath warm against her ear. "I'll be with you. No matter what. You don't have to do this alone."

And in that moment, Vivienne realized something that had been buried deep inside her for years. She wasn't just running from her family. She was running from herself—from the part of her that had always believed that she was nothing more than a tool in their game. But now, with Ethan by her side, she could choose a different path. She could fight for the life she deserved. And that fight, no matter how terrifying, was one she was finally ready to face.

"I choose us," she whispered, the words slipping from her lips as though they had been waiting to be spoken for a lifetime. "I choose us."

Ethan's arms tightened around her, and she felt the world shift beneath them. She didn't know what would happen next, but for the first time in her life, she felt like she had control. She wasn't running anymore. She was choosing. Choosing her future, choosing her freedom, and choosing the life that was truly hers.

Thirteen

The Shadows Linger

The cold wind rustled through the trees as Vivienne stepped out of her cottage, the faint glow of the streetlights casting long, stretching shadows along the path. The night had fallen with an oppressive stillness, the kind that made everything feel like it was holding its breath, waiting for something to happen. It was in this silence that Vivienne found herself, caught between the world she had tried to leave behind and the future she wasn't yet ready to embrace.

She had made the decision. She had chosen Ethan. She had chosen to fight for a life of her own, free from the weight of her family's expectations. But with each passing moment, as the world around her held its breath, Vivienne couldn't help but feel the uncertainty pressing in on all sides. Was she really ready to face the consequences of her choices? Could she really leave everything behind, even the family that had shaped her, even the legacy that had once felt like an unbreakable bond?

Ethan's words echoed in her mind, steady and sure: I'll be with you, no matter what. She had chosen him. She had chosen this new life, this fight for freedom. But she had no illusions about how difficult it would be. The road ahead was not just uncertain—it was treacherous.

The sound of footsteps behind her broke through her thoughts. Vivienne turned to find Ethan walking toward her, his figure emerging from the shadows like a ghost, his presence both familiar and grounding. Her heart gave a flutter at the sight of him, but the gnawing uncertainty didn't fade. If anything, it deepened.

"Are you sure about this?" Ethan's voice was calm, but there was an underlying current of concern, a question he had asked so many times before. He had always known the stakes, had always known that this wasn't just about love. It was about survival—surviving the pull of the past, surviving the consequences of their decisions.

Vivienne swallowed hard, meeting his gaze. She had known this moment would come, had known he would ask her to confirm what they had already agreed upon. But the weight of her answer still felt like a mountain.

"I'm sure," she said, her voice steadier than she felt. She had to be. She couldn't second-guess herself now, not when she had finally made the choice to fight for what she wanted. Not when she had finally chosen herself.

Ethan stepped closer, his eyes searching hers. The intensity in his gaze made her heart race, but it was the gentleness in his expression that grounded her, made her believe in this decision, made her believe in them.

"I've been thinking," he said softly, his words almost too quiet in the stillness of the night. "If we're going to do this, we have to do it all the way. We can't half-step into this, Vivienne. We can't run from this, or hide from what it means. You have to be ready for everything."

Vivienne nodded, her eyes never leaving his. She didn't have all the answers. She didn't know exactly what would come next, but one thing was certain: she couldn't turn back now. Not after everything that had happened, not after making the decision to finally live life on her terms.

"I'm ready," she said again, more firmly this time. "I'm ready to face whatever comes."

Ethan held her gaze for a long moment, then nodded. Without another word, he reached for her hand, his fingers entwining with hers in a silent promise. Together, they stood there for a moment, the weight of their unspoken bond filling the space between them.

"We have to leave tonight," he said, his voice low. "There's no more time to waste. They're already on to us, Vivienne. Your family. They know something's changed. They won't wait much longer."

Vivienne's breath caught in her throat. She had known the risk, had known the danger they were walking into, but hearing it from Ethan's lips made it feel so real, so immediate. The choice was no longer theoretical. They had to move now, or the consequences would be irreversible.

"I don't know if I can do this, Ethan," she admitted, her voice soft but filled with a raw honesty she hadn't expected to hear from herself. "I don't know if I'm strong enough to walk away from everything. From them."

Ethan's hand tightened around hers, pulling her toward him. "You are," he said, his voice steady and unwavering. "You've been strong your whole life, Vivienne. You've just been living for the wrong reasons. You've been living for them. For the people who made you believe that you couldn't be anything else. But you can. You can be anything you want."

His words were like a lifeline, like a tether pulling her away from the life she had known and toward something new, something unknown but full of possibility. The fear was still there, gnawing at her, but it was now accompanied by something else: hope.

"I'm scared," she whispered, the admission escaping her before she could stop it. "Scared of what will happen when we leave. Scared of what they'll do. Scared of what I'll become."

Ethan cupped her face in his hands, his thumbs brushing across her skin in soothing strokes. "You don't have to be scared, Vivienne. Whatever happens, we'll face it together. I won't let you face this alone."

The truth of his words sank in deep, warming her from the inside out. He wasn't offering her promises he couldn't keep. He was offering her something far more important: partnership. The chance to build a life with someone who truly understood the stakes, someone who wouldn't back down when things got hard.

And for the first time, Vivienne realized that she didn't have to be afraid anymore. She didn't have to fight this battle alone.

"Okay," she said softly, looking into Ethan's eyes, letting the resolve settle in her chest. "Let's do this."

They didn't waste any more time. Together, they made their way out of the small town, walking in the shadow of the night, as though they were both stepping into a future neither of them could fully predict. The weight of the decision, the weight of everything they were leaving behind, sat heavy in her chest, but it wasn't a burden anymore. It was a choice, a choice that she had made with her own two hands.

As they walked, side by side, toward the unknown, Vivienne couldn't help but think of everything she had left behind. Her family. The business empire that had defined her existence. The life she had once thought was her only option. But none of it mattered anymore. She had chosen something else. She had chosen Ethan. She had chosen freedom.

The town faded behind them, its lights growing dimmer with

each step, until it was nothing more than a shadow in the distance. The night was their only companion, the only certainty in a world that had suddenly become too big to understand, too full of questions to be answered.

When they reached the outskirts of the town, Ethan stopped. He turned to her, his face serious but filled with something softer beneath the surface.

"This is it," he said, his voice quiet. "Once we leave, there's no going back. Your family won't let this go. You know that, right?"

Vivienne nodded, her heart pounding in her chest. She knew the consequences. She knew the risks. But it didn't matter anymore. She had made her choice.

"I'm ready," she whispered again, the words feeling stronger now, more certain.

Ethan pulled her into his arms, holding her tightly for a moment. She could feel his heartbeat, steady and strong against hers, and in that moment, she knew that they were more than just two people fighting for a chance at happiness. They were fighting for their lives, fighting to be seen for who they truly were, not for who others wanted them to be.

"I'll never let go," Ethan said, his voice a promise.

And as they turned together, heading toward the road that stretched out before them, Vivienne knew that the rift between the life she had known and the life she was choosing had finally closed. The world they were stepping into might be filled with uncertainty, but for the first time in her life, Vivienne didn't fear the unknown. She embraced it, because with Ethan by her side, there was nothing they couldn't face together.

This was their moment. The beginning of their future. And no matter what came next, it would be a life of their own choosing. And that was enough.

Fourteen

Letting Go

The first days after they left the town felt like a dream. It was as though the world had shifted around them, as though time itself had reset, giving Vivienne and Ethan a clean slate. But no matter how much they tried to build their new life, no matter how much they tried to distance themselves from the past, the shadows followed them.

The road ahead was long, but the silence between them was even longer. They hadn't spoken about what they had done. They hadn't spoken about the life they had chosen to leave behind. It was as if they both knew there was no going back to that world, that world of expectations and lies, but still, there was a distance between them—an unspoken fear, an invisible barrier neither of them knew how to breach.

They had crossed state lines, and every mile that put them

Letting Go

farther away from the life they had known should have felt like a triumph, but Vivienne couldn't shake the feeling of unease that had settled in her chest. It wasn't just the uncertainty of their future that weighed on her. It was something deeper, something she couldn't articulate even to herself.

They had stayed in motels, small towns that seemed to appear out of nowhere and then disappear just as quickly. There was no time for rest. No time for them to stop moving. It felt like they were running again, but this time, it wasn't just from the life she had left behind. It was from everything. From the decisions that had brought them here, from the people who would never understand.

But the truth was, Vivienne couldn't escape her family. No matter how far she ran, they were still a part of her—like a weight tied around her ankles, pulling her down into the depths of a past she would never be free from. And she had known, deep down, that her family wouldn't let her go that easily. She had known the price of defying them. But she had never imagined it would come at the cost of Ethan.

Her thoughts were interrupted by a sharp knock on the motel room door. The sound jolted her out of her haze, and she turned to Ethan, who was standing by the window, his eyes scanning the parking lot below. There was a tense air about him, a feeling of urgency that hadn't been there before. He was already moving toward the door before she could say anything.

"Stay back," he whispered, his voice low, urgent. "I'll handle it."

Vivienne's heart pounded in her chest as she stepped away from the door, her pulse quickening. The knock had been too deliberate, too forceful to be a coincidence. Someone was looking for them. She didn't know who, but the familiar weight of dread settled into her stomach, twisting it into knots.

Ethan glanced over his shoulder at her, his face a mask of calm, but there was something in his eyes—a flicker of something—she couldn't ignore.

"I'll be fine," he said, his voice steady but tinged with an edge that wasn't there before. "Just stay here."

Before she could protest, Ethan opened the door, and Vivienne's heart stopped as she saw the figure standing in the doorway.

It wasn't a stranger. It was someone she knew. Someone she hadn't seen in years.

Her mother.

The woman stood there, her posture rigid, her face hard as steel. Vivienne could see the anger and hurt in her eyes, the years of resentment that had always been there but were now impossible to mask. Her mother's gaze flickered over to Vivienne, but it was Ethan she focused on.

"I should have known," her mother said coldly, her voice slicing through the tension in the air. "You think you can run away from all of this? From your responsibilities? From your family?"

Letting Go

Vivienne felt the blood drain from her face. Her mother's presence was like a storm cloud, dark and overwhelming. She had thought she could escape it, had thought that by leaving everything behind, she could outrun the years of manipulation, the years of being groomed for a life she never asked for. But here she was. Here they both were.

"You don't get to make these decisions for me anymore," Vivienne said, her voice shaking but filled with a newfound determination. She had chosen this. She had chosen Ethan. And for the first time in her life, she wasn't going to let her family control her.

Her mother's lips curled into a cold, humorless smile. "You really think you can just walk away from this? From us?" she sneered, her voice filled with venom. "You're a part of this family, Vivienne. You don't get to just leave, no matter how far you run."

Ethan stepped forward, his hand resting on Vivienne's shoulder, as if offering her some silent support. "This isn't about your family anymore," he said, his voice calm but firm. "Vivienne made her choice. We're not going back."

Vivienne's mother turned her icy gaze on Ethan, her eyes narrowing as if she were sizing him up. She didn't even acknowledge him, as though he were beneath her. "I know exactly who you are," she said, her tone low. "And I know exactly what you're doing. You think you can protect her from what's coming? You think you can shield her from the consequences?"

Ethan didn't flinch. "We'll face whatever comes. Together."

But Vivienne's mother wasn't done. She took a step closer, her eyes now locking onto Vivienne with an intensity that made her stomach twist. "You think this man will save you? You think this love—whatever you want to call it—will protect you from what's coming? You're playing a game, Vivienne. And you're about to lose."

Vivienne felt the sharp sting of her mother's words, but she didn't let it show. She had already lost so much, but she wasn't going to lose herself. Not now. Not after everything she had fought for.

"I'm not a part of this anymore," Vivienne said, her voice filled with the conviction she had been searching for all her life. "I'm done living by your rules. I'm done with the lies, the manipulation, the expectations. I'm not going back."

Her mother's eyes flared with anger, but there was something more there now—something darker. "You think you're free? You think you've escaped?" She laughed, but it was empty, hollow. "You've never been free, Vivienne. And neither is he."

Vivienne's heart dropped at her mother's words. She didn't know what it meant, but she knew it wasn't good. She knew there was more to her mother's presence than just an attempt to bring her back into the fold. This was something bigger. Something more dangerous.

"Get out," Vivienne said, her voice steady despite the rising panic in her chest. She was done with this. Done with the past. Done with the people who had held her captive in their world for so long.

Her mother didn't move at first. There was a long silence, the air thick with unspoken words, before she finally stepped back, her expression a mixture of disbelief and contempt.

"You'll regret this, Vivienne," she said, her voice cold. "And when you do, don't come crawling back. You won't find me there. You'll find nothing."

With that, she turned and walked away, her heels clicking sharply against the floor, the sound echoing in the silence left behind. The door slammed shut behind her, and Vivienne felt the weight of the moment crash down on her.

For a long time, neither she nor Ethan spoke. The room was suffocating in its silence, the tension between them palpable.

Finally, Ethan turned to her, his eyes softening. "You don't have to carry this alone," he said, his voice barely a whisper.

Vivienne didn't answer immediately. She was too overwhelmed, too shaken by her mother's presence and the words she had left behind. The threat that lingered in the air wasn't just a threat against her. It was a threat against Ethan, against their future. And Vivienne couldn't help but wonder: how much would they have to pay for the love they had chosen?

"I'm not going back," she whispered finally, her voice steady despite the terror creeping at the edges of her heart. "I'm not going to let them control me anymore. But I don't know if I'm strong enough to fight this on my own."

Ethan moved closer, taking her hand in his. "You're not alone," he said, his voice filled with determination. "We'll face whatever comes, together. I won't let them take you from me. And I won't let them take you from yourself."

And for the first time in what felt like forever, Vivienne believed him. She didn't know what the future held, or what price they would have to pay for the life they had chosen, but she knew one thing for sure: she would never walk alone again.

The cost of love was high, but she was ready to pay it. And whatever came next, she would face it, side by side with Ethan, with the strength of a love that was finally hers to claim.

Fifteen

Embracing Her True Self

The silence in the motel room was almost unbearable—the kind that hung in the air like a thick fog, smothering everything around it. Vivienne could hear the distant hum of passing cars on the highway outside, but it felt like those sounds were miles away, as though they were part of another life—one that she wasn't a part of anymore.

Ethan sat at the small table by the window, his back to her, staring into the night. The room was dimly lit, the only light coming from the flickering neon sign outside. The moment her mother had left, the world had shifted in ways Vivienne hadn't anticipated. Her mother's warning echoed in her ears, like a threat waiting to come to life.

You'll regret this, Vivienne. And when you do, don't come crawling back. You won't find me there. You'll find nothing.

She closed her eyes, trying to shake off the lingering fear that had taken root in her chest. She had made her choice. She had chosen Ethan, chosen to walk away from the life her family had crafted for her. But was it the right choice? Would it be the choice that set them both free, or the one that tore them apart?

Vivienne pushed the thought away, shaking her head. No. She couldn't second-guess herself now. She had chosen, and now, they had to live with it.

She stood and moved toward Ethan, her footsteps soft against the worn carpet. She could see the tension in his shoulders, the way his hands were clenched into fists on the table. The same tension she felt in herself, like an electric charge in the air, waiting for something to snap.

"Ethan?" she said softly, her voice unsure.

He didn't turn around right away, and for a moment, Vivienne wondered if he had heard her at all. Then, slowly, he turned to face her. His expression was unreadable, his eyes distant in a way that unsettled her.

"What's going on?" she asked, her heart aching at the sight of him. She had never seen him like this—so withdrawn, so guarded. Was this the man she had chosen to build her life with? Or was it someone else entirely, someone she had never really known?

Ethan exhaled slowly, as if weighing the words in his mind before he spoke. "I've been thinking about what your mother said," he began, his voice quiet but heavy with meaning. "About what's coming next. We can't hide from this forever, Vivienne. They won't stop looking for us. Your family won't stop until they drag you back into their world."

Vivienne flinched at the words. The truth of them cut deeper than she had expected. She had always known, in the back of her mind, that walking away from her family wouldn't be easy. But hearing it from Ethan made it real, made it feel like the walls were closing in around them.

"I don't want to go back," she said firmly, her voice stronger than she felt. "I don't care what they do. I've made my choice. I'm not going back."

Ethan's eyes softened, but there was something in them that made Vivienne's heart ache. It was fear, mixed with something else—something she couldn't quite put her finger on.

"I'm not saying we go back," he said slowly, as though choosing his words carefully. "But we can't keep running forever either. The moment we left, we set something in motion. And we have to deal with the consequences of that decision. The longer we hide, the more dangerous it gets. Your family… they won't stop until they get what they want."

Vivienne took a step closer, her gaze fixed on him. She couldn't let him pull away from her—not now. "What are you saying, Ethan? What do we do now?"

He stood up from the table, moving toward her with slow,

deliberate steps. When he reached her, he reached out to touch her face, his fingers soft against her skin. "I'm saying we need to face them," he said quietly. "We need to confront your family head-on. It's the only way to stop them from tearing us apart."

Vivienne's breath caught in her throat. She hadn't expected this. She hadn't expected him to suggest something so bold, so dangerous. Confronting her family was a death sentence, in a way. It would be the end of any semblance of peace they had built. The end of their quiet life.

But as she looked into Ethan's eyes, something in her stirred—a kind of clarity that she hadn't expected. Ethan was right. She couldn't keep running. No matter how far they went, no matter how many miles they put between themselves and the past, her family's reach would always be there, pulling at her, dragging her back into the world she had fled.

"You're right," she said, her voice steady now. "We can't run anymore. But we can't just walk into the lion's den without a plan."

Ethan nodded, his fingers still lightly caressing her cheek. "I know. But we have to act fast. They'll come for us, Vivienne. They'll come for you. And I won't let them take you without a fight."

Vivienne closed her eyes at the words, feeling the weight of them settle in her chest. She had already made one choice that had set this all in motion. Now, she was faced with another: to face her family and the consequences of walking away, or to continue running, knowing it would never truly end.

"Okay," she said finally, her voice firm. "We'll do it. We'll face them together."

Ethan's grip on her tightened, his eyes searching hers for something—some sign that she was truly ready for what they were about to do. For what it would cost them. For the battle they would have to fight.

"Are you sure?" he asked softly, his voice filled with concern. "This isn't just about you anymore, Vivienne. It's about both of us. About everything we've built."

"I'm sure," she replied, her voice strong, unyielding. "We've already chosen this. There's no turning back."

For a long moment, they stood there, locked in a shared understanding, the weight of their decision hanging heavy in the air. Vivienne's heart thundered in her chest, and yet, she felt a sense of calm settle over her. This was it. This was the moment when everything changed. The moment when they would either fall or rise, depending on the choices they made.

Ethan kissed her then, a soft, gentle kiss that held all the unspoken promises between them. The promise of a life they could create together. The promise of freedom, no matter the cost.

When they pulled away, his eyes were filled with something she hadn't seen before—a deep, unshakable resolve. "Let's get ready," he said, his voice low. "We don't have much time. They'll be here soon."

Vivienne nodded, taking a deep breath as she stepped back from him. The plan had been set in motion. They would face her family. They would confront the empire that had controlled her life, the people who had shaped her every decision.

But she wasn't doing it alone. She wasn't alone in this fight anymore. With Ethan by her side, she could face whatever came next.

As they gathered their things, as they prepared for the storm that was about to hit, Vivienne realized something: this wasn't just about facing her family. It was about facing herself. About proving to herself that she could fight for the life she wanted, not the one they had chosen for her.

She wasn't just running anymore. She was fighting. Fighting for her future. Fighting for her freedom. Fighting for a love that was finally hers to claim.

The sound of the door opening interrupted her thoughts, and she turned to see Ethan standing in the doorway, his expression filled with the same sense of determination she felt.

"We're in this together," he said quietly, his voice steady.

Vivienne nodded, her heart swelling with something close to relief. They had chosen this. They had chosen each other. And now, together, they would face whatever came next.

Embracing Her True Self

The road ahead was uncertain. But for the first time, Vivienne felt like she had the power to shape it. And she wasn't afraid. Because with Ethan beside her, there was nothing they couldn't face. Nothing that could tear them apart.

No matter the cost.

www.ingramcontent.com/pod-product-compliance
Lightning Source LLC
LaVergne TN
LVHW010551070526
838199LV00063BA/4941